W9-DEU-495

Country File
Great Britain

Clare Oliver

Smart Apple Media

First published in 2001 by Franklin Watts
96 Leonard Street, London EC2A 4XD, UK

Franklin Watts Australia
56 O'Riordan Street, Alexandria, NSW 2015

Country File: Great Britain produced for Franklin Watts by
Bender Richardson White, PO Box 266, Uxbridge, UK.

Project Editor: Lionel Bender, Text Editor: Peter
Harrison, Designer: Ben White, Picture Researcher:
Cathy Stastny, Media Conversion and Make-up:
Mike Pilley/Radius, Production: Kim Richardson
Graphics: Mike Pilley/Radius, Maps: Stefan Chabluk
Copyright © 2001 Bender Richardson White

For Franklin Watts, Series Editor: Adrian Cole, Art
Director: Jonathan Hair

Published in the United States by Smart Apple Media
1980 Lookout Drive, North Mankato, MN 56003

Library of Congress Cataloging-in-Publication Data

Oliver, Clare.
Great Britain / by Clare Oliver.
p. cm. — (Country files)
Includes index.
Summary: An introduction to the geography,
government, economy, culture, and people of Great
Britain.
ISBN 1-58340-204-7
1. Great Britain—Juvenile literature. [1. Great Britain.]
I. Title. II. Series.

DA27.5 .O55 2002
941—dc21   2002017027

9 8 7 6 5 4 3 2 1

Picture Credits

Pages: 1: PhotoDisc Inc./Jeremy Hoare. 3: PhotoDisc
Inc./Andrew Ward/Life File. 4: PhotoDisc Inc/Colin
Paterson. 6: Hutchison Photo Library/Robert Francis.
8: Hutchison Photo Library/Jeremy Horner.
9: Hutchison Photo Library/Peter Morzynski. 10 top:
PhotoDisc Inc./Andrew Ward/Life File. 10–11 bottom:
PhotoDisc Inc./Jeremy Hoare. 12 DAS Photo/David
Simson. 14–15 bottom: Hutchison Photo Library.
16–17: Eye Ubiquitous/G. Daniels. 18 top: John
Walmsley Photography. 18 bottom: Ted Spiegal/Corbis
Images. 20: Hutchison Photo Library/Bernard Gérard.
21: Eye Ubiquitous/Martin Foyle. 22: Hutchison Photo
Library/Bernard Gérard. 23: PhotoDisc Inc./Andrew
Ward/Life File. 24: Peter Tumley/Corbis Images.
26: PhotoDisc Inc./Andrew Ward/Life File. 28: Reuters
NewMedia Inc./Corbis Images. 29: Howard Davis/Corbis
Images. 30: PhotoDisc Inc./John Wang. 31: PhotoDisc
Inc./Andrew Ward/Life File.
Cover photo: James Davis Travel Photography.

The Author

Clare Oliver is a full-time writer and
editor of nonfiction books. She has
written more than 50 books for
children. This is her second book
about Great Britain.

Contents

Welcome to Great Britain

Great Britain is made up of the kingdoms of England and Scotland and the principality of Wales. Together with the province of Northern Ireland, it is part of the United Kingdom (UK). The UK is a member of the European Union (EU).

The mainland of Great Britain is one of the two largest islands to the west of continental Europe. The other island is Ireland, where the British province of Northern Ireland is situated. Several island groups and thousands of smaller islands are also part of Great Britain.

Worldwide influence

Great Britain is famous as the birthplace of the Industrial Revolution. It was the first nation in the world to shift from an economy based on agriculture to one based on industry and manufacturing. Despite its small land area, Great Britain controlled a large colonial empire until the early 20th century. It still plays a key role in global events. The nation's principal language, English, is now a world language of business and culture.

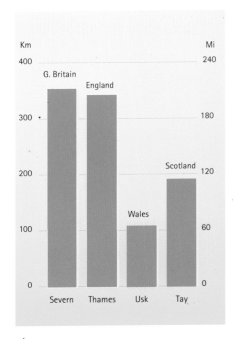

▲ The length of Britain's longest rivers. The river Severn runs through England and Wales.

Eilean Donan Castle in the Scottish Highlands has been a fortified site for 800 years. The present castle dates from the early 20th century. ▼▼

12°W 10°W 8°W 6°W 4°W 2°W 0° 2°E

SHETLAND
ISLANDS

Fair Isle

ORKNEY
ISLANDS

Lewis

OUTER
HEBRIDES

St. Kilda

Skye

Mull

Inverness

Spey

Don

Dee

GRAMPIAN MTS.

Oban

Tay

Dundee

Montrose

Fraserburgh
Peterhead
Aberdeen

ATLANTIC

OCEAN

Islay

Forth

Perth

Glasgow

Clyde

Edinburgh

Tweed

Holy I.

Ayr

SCOTLAND

Arran

CHEVIOT HILLS

NORTH

SEA

Stranraer

Newcastle upon Tyne

Carlisle

Tyne

Durham

LAKE
DISTRICT

Middlesbrough

Londonderry
NORTHERN
IRELAND

Lough
Neagh

Belfast

Armagh

Isle of
Man

Douglas

IRISH

SEA

Preston

Leeds

Hull

Manchester

Liverpool

Sheffield

Holyhead

The
Wash

REPUBLIC

OF

IRELAND

SNOWDONIA

Wrexham

Derby

Trent

ENGLAND

Norwich

ST. GEORGES CHANNEL

Cardigan
Bay

Aberystwyth

Wolverhampton

Birmingham

Coventry

Peterborough

Cambridge
Ipswich

Wye

Severn

Northampton

Colchester

WALES

Carmarthen

COTSWOLD HILLS

Oxford

London

Swansea

Cardiff

Bristol

Thames

Canterbury

Bristol Channel

Salisbury

Folkestone

Dover

Lundy

Southampton

Brighton

Exeter

Bournemouth

Isle of
Wight

DARTMOOR

Plymouth

N
W   E
S

Penzance

ISLES OF
SCILLY

ENGLISH CHANNEL

Alderney

CHANNEL ISLANDS

Guernsey

Jersey

FRANCE

5

The Land

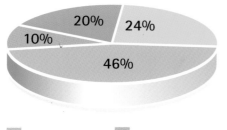

Permanent Pastures   ■ Forests and Woodland

■ Other   ■ Arable Land

▲
▲ Land use in Great Britain.

Typical landscape in southern England—
rolling hills, fields, hedges, trees, and a
country house. ▼

The British landscape varies from green, rolling hills to steep mountains. A mild, wet climate keeps much of the land fertile.

The wettest places are mountainous western regions, such as the Highlands of Scotland, the Lake District in northwest England, and Snowdonia in north Wales. These all receive more than 12 inches (3,000 mm) of rain each year. The east is much drier, and some places there average less than three inches (700 mm) of rain in a year.

The Highlands include Britain's highest peak, Ben Nevis (4,406 feet (1,343 m)). Deep lakes, called lochs, fill the Highland valleys. The part of Scotland called the Central Lowlands consists of low, rolling hills. Watered by the rivers Clyde, Forth, and Tay, it is mostly farmland.

A varied landscape and climate

The land rises again near the Scottish border, first with the Southern Upland range, and then the Cheviot Hills. Northern England is rugged and bleak and includes Cumbria's mountainous Lake District. The region features England's highest peak, Scafell Pike (3,209 feet (978 m)).

The Pennines run like a spine from northern England to the region known as the Midlands, which is dominated by the valleys of the Severn, Trent, and Avon Rivers. Central and eastern England are mostly made up of low plains. There are chalk hills called downs in the south, and rugged moors and rocky coasts to the southwest.

The Welsh landscape includes, in the north, Britain's second-highest peak, Mount Snowdon (3,560 feet (1,085 m)), and in the south, the mountainous Brecon Beacons.

The average annual temperature in Great Britain ranges from about 44 °F (7 °C) on the island of Shetland, to about 52 °F (11 °C) on the Cornish coast.

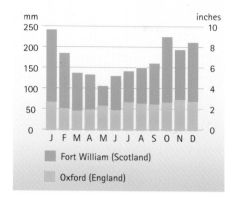

▲ Annual rainfall comparison between towns in Scotland and England.

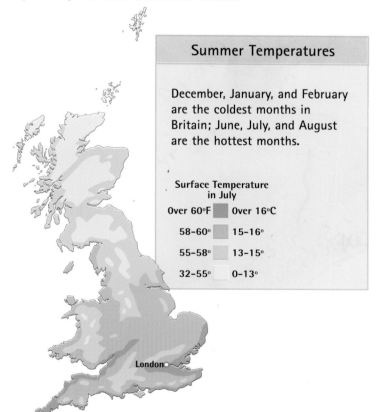

Summer Temperatures

December, January, and February are the coldest months in Britain; June, July, and August are the hottest months.

Surface Temperature in July

Over 60°F	Over 16°C
58–60°	15–16°
55–58°	13–15°
32–55°	0–13°

London

Animal Life

Great Britain's mammals include deer, squirrels, a species of mole, badgers, foxes, rabbits, hares, mice, and bats.

Among reptiles and amphibians are lizards, frogs, newts, and toads, but snakes are unknown in most places except the south and southeast.

Birdlife includes several types of gulls, ducks, geese, tits, and swans, as well as ptarmigan, golden eagles, and gray herons.

Web Search ▶▶

▶ www.met-office.gov.uk
The website of British weather.

The People

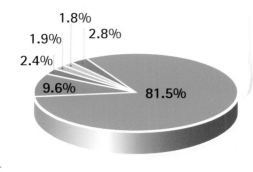

1.8%
1.9%
2.8%
2.4%
9.6%
81.5%

English | Scottish | Irish | Welsh
Ulster | West Indian, Indian, Pakistani, and others

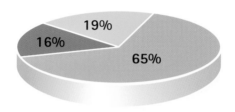

▲ British people by ethnic groups.

Despite its small land area, Britain is home to just over 57 million people. As well as the native Scots, Welsh, and English, many other ethnic groups have settled in Britain over the centuries.

Scottish people account for nearly 10 percent of the population. Less than two percent of the population are Welsh. The Scots and Welsh are descendants of the Celts, who settled the islands in prehistoric times. The English, who make up 82 percent of the population, take their name from the Angles, a Germanic tribe that arrived in the fifth and sixth centuries A.D.

After World War II, people from former British colonies such as India, Hong Kong, and the West Indies were encouraged to come to Britain to help re-establish the workforce. People from non-native ethnic groups now account for about five percent of the total population.

19%
16%
65%

Age 0–14: 11.2 million (Male 5.8 m/Female 5.5 m)
Age 15–64: 38.5 million (Male 19.4 m/Female 19.1 m)
Age 65+: 9.2 million (Male 3.8 m/Female 5.4 m)

▲ Population by age and sex.

Language and age

The official language of Great Britain is English. About 26 percent of people in Wales speak Welsh. Scots Gaelic is spoken by about 60,000 people. Ethnic communities often keep alive their native languages by using them when talking in their homes.

At Speakers' Corner in London, anyone —of any culture, ethnic group, religion, or nationality—can speak openly. ▼

The birth rate and death rate are low, as a result of good living standards. Men live to around 74 years of age and women to about 80. Overall, the population is gradually aging. More than 16 percent of people are over the age of 65, and this figure will rise to about 20 percent by 2021.

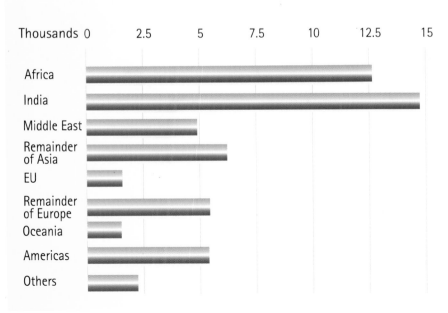

Immigrants given British citizenship in 2000.

Thousands 0   2.5   5   7.5   10   12.5   15

- Africa
- India
- Middle East
- Remainder of Asia
- EU
- Remainder of Europe
- Oceania
- Americas
- Others

 The southeast is the most heavily populated region. Here, commuters in London wait to get on an urban train.

 Web Search ►►

► **www.statistics.gov.uk**
Up-to-the-minute facts and figures about Great Britain and the United Kingdom.

► **www.open.gov.uk**
www.wales.gov.uk
www.scotland.net
www.discovernorthern ireland.com
Information on all parts of Britain and the United Kingdom .

▲▲ In rural areas, traditional homes range from small cottages like these to large country estates.

Population Density

Because of its relatively small size compared to its population, Great Britain has one of the world's highest population densities.

Population—people
per sq mi/km

2,600 or over		1000 or over	
1500–2600		600–999	
780–1500		300–599	
390–780		150–299	
under 390		under 150	

Edinburgh

Manchester

Birmingham

Cardiff   London

Urban and Rural Life

Almost 650 people live in each square mile (250 per sq km) of Great Britain, more than twice as many as in neighboring France. Over 90 percent of British people live in towns and cities.

As cities have become more crowded, many people have chosen to commute into the city. As a result, once-tiny villages and towns have sprawled outwards with new housing developments and shopping areas.

Building new houses and converting old ones

Rows of red-brick townhouses are a common sight in the industrial cities that thrived in the late-19th and early-20th centuries. Many grew up around coalfields in south Wales and in England's northeast. During the 1950s and 1960s, blocks of government-owned apartments were built to fill areas devastated by World War II bombing. By the late 20th century, government tenants were encouraged to buy their properties: the number of occupant-owned houses and apartments increased from 49 percent in 1970 to 67.3 percent by 2000.

Many large, old family homes, particularly in cities such as London, have been converted into apartments for people to buy or rent. In recent years, new housing, offices, and malls have been built in the abandoned dockyards of major cities, including Liverpool and Edinburgh.

◄◄ Traffic in London, which is the largest city in Great Britain. It has a population of over 7 million.

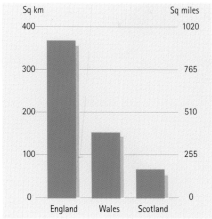

▲ Population density.

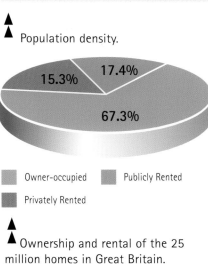

Owner-occupied Publicly Rented
Privately Rented

▲ Ownership and rental of the 25 million homes in Great Britain.

Web Search ►►

► www.streetmap.co.uk
Find and print a streetmap of any British town or village.

► www.housing.detr.gov.uk/information
Statistics on houses and homes.

Farming and Fishing

British farming and fishing are highly mechanized, although in Wales and Scotland there are still small farms. Generally, the lowland areas of Britain have rich soil that is good for arable farming. In the hills and mountains, plentiful rainfall keeps the grass green for grazing animals.

The most important crops are cereals (wheat, barley, and oats), oilseed rape, sugarbeet, and potatoes. Some of these are grown as animal feed. There are fruit farms and market gardens in areas such as Kent, in southeast England.

Sheep and cattle are the most numerous livestock, followed by pigs and poultry. Wales, in particular, is famous for its lamb and mutton. Scotland is famous for its Aberdeen Angus, a hardy breed of beef cattle, but most cattle are part of dairy herds. Dairy products include milk, butter, and a wide range of cheeses, most famously English Cheddar and Stilton.

A small fishing boat in harbor. ▼
▼

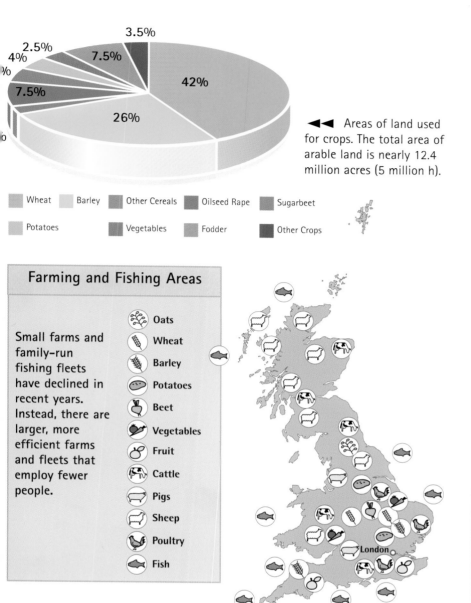

42%

26%

7.5%

4%

2.5%

7.5%

3.5%

Wheat · Barley · Other Cereals · Oilseed Rape · Sugarbeet
Potatoes · Vegetables · Fodder · Other Crops

◀◀ Areas of land used for crops. The total area of arable land is nearly 12.4 million acres (5 million h).

Farming and Fishing Areas

Small farms and family-run fishing fleets have declined in recent years. Instead, there are larger, more efficient farms and fleets that employ fewer people.

Oats
Wheat
Barley
Potatoes
Beet
Vegetables
Fruit
Cattle
Pigs
Sheep
Poultry
Fish

London

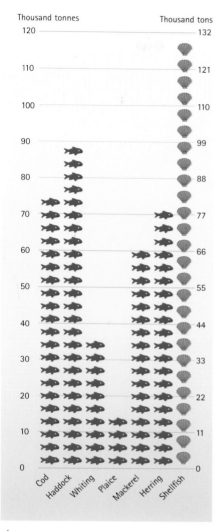

Thousand tonnes   Thousand tons

▲ Fish catches per year made by Great Britain's seagoing boats.

The fishing industry

The British fishing fleet numbers more than 8,000 vessels. They land over 661,500 tons (600,000 t) of seafish a year, more than 65 percent of the country's needs.

Intensive overfishing has reduced the numbers of fish caught and, when Britain became part of the European Community (now the EU), it agreed not to fish beyond 200 miles (320 km) from its coast. In spite of this, the Dogger Bank in the North Sea remains one of the world's richest fishing grounds. Chief catches are cod, haddock, whiting, mackerel, turbot, herring, and plaice.

Web Search ▶▶

▶ www.maff.gov.uk
Details of farming and fishing from the Ministry of Agriculture, Fisheries, and Food.

Resources and Industry

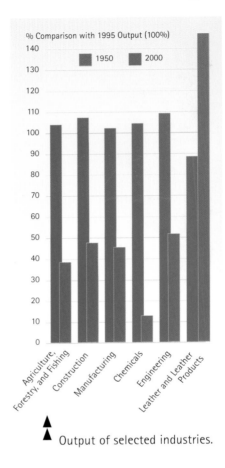

% Comparison with 1995 Output (100%)

■ 1950 ■ 2000

(Bar chart with values: 140, 130, 120, 110, 100, 90, 80, 70, 60, 50, 40, 30, 20, 10, 0)

Agriculture, Forestry, and Fishing | Construction | Manufacturing | Chemicals | Engineering | Leather and Leather Products

Output of selected industries.

Britain is one of the top industrial countries in the world. Although the reserves of iron and coal that fueled its development have declined, British industry still contributes about 25 percent of the country's gross domestic product (GDP).

Britain produces 110 million tons (100 million t) of coal each year, mostly to be burned in power stations. As a result of the oil and gas reserves discovered in the North Sea, Britain has more energy resources than any other EU country. Other mineral resources include tin and zinc, and quarries supply sand, gravel, and limestone.

Manufacturing

Electronics, cars, and aerospace equipment dominate manufacturing. Factories also make chemicals (especially medicines), man-made fibers, plastics, and furniture. Sheffield steel and silver are world-famous. Other industries include food, drinks, and tobacco, printing and publishing, and the "rag trade" (clothing). Overall, manufacturing employs over 20 percent of the workforce.

All kinds of services

Service industries include computer support, insurance, and management consulting. These industries have taken over from manufacturing as the major employers, with 65 percent of all workers. They are also the biggest and fastest-growing, with expansion occurring in shops, restaurants, travel agents, fitness centers, and finance. The London Stock Exchange helps make Britain one of the world's major financial centers.

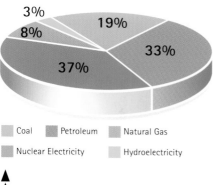

3% 8% 19% 33% 37%

Coal   Petroleum   Natural Gas
Nuclear Electricity   Hydroelectricity

▲▲ Energy consumption in 2000.

Fossil Fuels and Industry

Deposits of coal, oil and natural gas—all fossil fuels—are found mostly in the north and offshore. The little manufacturing that remains is located mainly in the Midlands and northeast. The service industries are concentrated in the southeast.

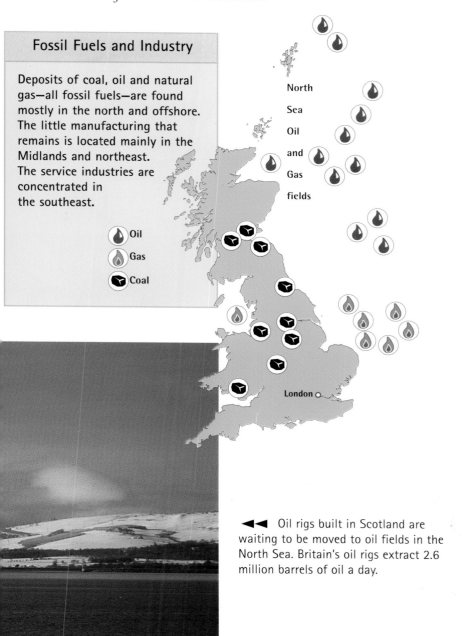

🛢 Oil
🛢 Gas
⚙ Coal

North
Sea
Oil
and
Gas
fields

London ○

Major Changes

The last 25 years have seen dramatic changes in British energy production and use. Since 1975, output of crude oil has increased 80 times, coal production has more than halved, and output of natural gas and nuclear electricity have tripled.

Britain uses only 10 percent more energy today than it did in 1975, but the output of its industries has doubled. Its use of energy is far more efficient. Power stations also produce far less pollution. Britain's anti-pollution measures are among the best in the world.

Web Search ▶▶

▶ www.dti.gov.uk
The website of the nation's Department of Trade and Industry.

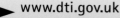

◀◀ Oil rigs built in Scotland are waiting to be moved to oil fields in the North Sea. Britain's oil rigs extract 2.6 million barrels of oil a day.

15

Transportation

Roads and highways are Britain's primary domestic transportation routes, although there is an extensive rail network and several internal air routes.

At the beginning of the 20th century, trains and canal barges were the main means of transporting heavy goods. Now, around 65 percent are carried by trucks. The biggest road-users are car drivers, and about 72 percent of households have at least one car. New roads have been built to accommodate the extra traffic, but gridlock is still a problem in many places during rush hours.

Some workers commute to work by train, although these services, too, are overstretched. Britain's rail network covers 10,354 miles (16,659 km). Various private rail companies operate the trains, and a central company called Railtrack maintains the tracks.

1%
1%   6%
6%
6%   86%

- Cars, Vans, and Taxis
- Buses and Coaches
- Other Road Traffic
- Rail Travel
- Domestic Flights

▲ Methods of transportation.

Britain has 27.5 million registered road vehicles, traveling on 2,053 miles (3,303 km) of highways and 231,200 miles (372,000 km) of public roads. ▼

Highways

The main highways run north to south. London is the hub of the highway network. The M25, opened in 1986, is a circular expressway that allows heavy traffic to bypass the city. Highways from London to Dover and Folkestone allow vehicles access to ferries and Channel Tunnel trains that connect with continental Europe.

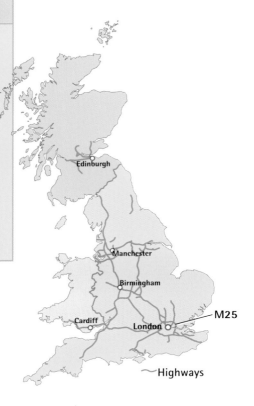

Edinburgh

Manchester

Birmingham

Cardiff

London

M25

Highways

Air and sea routes

Air traffic in Britain has increased dramatically in recent years. London has three main airports—Heathrow, Gatwick, and Stansted. Together with the airports at Glasgow, Manchester, Prestwick, and Aberdeen, these handle about 75 percent of passenger air traffic.

Shipping is the main form of cargo transportation into and out of Britain despite the opening of the Channel Tunnel to France in 1994. However, the number of people traveling by sea has declined. Ferries from Dover, the busiest seaport, carry passengers to mainland Europe.

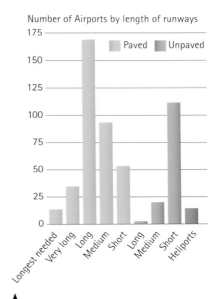

Number of Airports by length of runways

▲▲ Britain's airports and heliports. Heathrow is Europe's busiest airport; more than 60 million passengers pass through it each year.

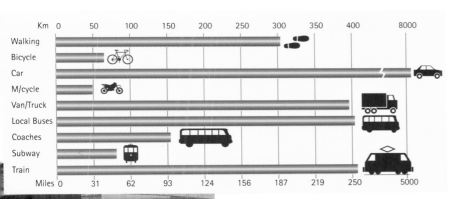

◄◄ Average yearly distances per person by type of travel.

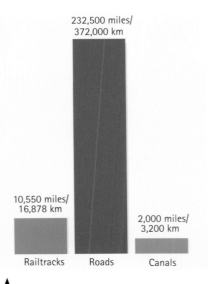

232,500 miles/
372,000 km

10,550 miles/
16,878 km

2,000 miles/
3,200 km

Railtracks   Roads   Canals

▲▲ Total length of roads, rail, and canals.

🌐 **Web Search** ►►

► **www.rail.co.uk**
Britain's railway companies, timetables, and travel services.

► **www.theaa.co.uk**
The Automobile Association.

► **www.caa.co.uk**
The Civil Aviation Association.

► **www.abports.co.uk**
The Association of British Ports.

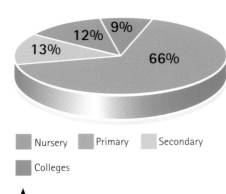

▲ In many secondary schools, children must wear a school uniform.

◄◄ Students relaxing outside King's College, Cambridge University, one of the oldest colleges in Britain. It dates from the 13th century.

9%

12%

13%

66%

Nursery   Primary   Secondary

Colleges

▲ Number of schools at all levels.

Education

British children must attend primary school from the age of five. At age 11 they attend secondary school until they are 16. Education is free for all children from 5 to 19, but about six percent of children pay tuition to go to private schools.

Children attend school from Monday to Friday and, in some private schools, on Saturday morning. The school year is up to 39 weeks long, usually divided into three terms. Since 1988 there has been a national curriculum for England and Wales. This means that all schools teach the same subjects at the same levels of difficulty. Scotland has its own curriculum system, but the subjects and topics taught are much the same.

From school to university

Children under the age of five do not have to go to school but may attend nursery from the age of three. Spaces are limited, but there are many private nurseries.

At age five, children begin primary school. Here, they are taught reading, writing, and math. They also study art, music, religious education, and computing. There are lessons in simple geography, history, and science.

Ninety-one percent of children over 11 go to a mixed-sex comprehensive school. For the first three years they study a range of subjects and begin at least one modern language. At age 14 or 15, they start to study for public exams, called GCSEs in England and Wales, or SSGs in Scotland. Children may then remain at school or study for A-Level exams, called Highers in Scotland.

Students are admitted to universities based on the A-Levels they pass. If students are unable to pay their tuition fees and living expenses themselves, they can get a government loan. Students in Scotland receive a grant.

DATABASE

TV Education

The Open University was set up in 1971. Its students are mostly adults who did not go on to higher education straight after school. They follow correspondence courses, allowing them to study and have a job at the same time. BBC television and radio programs back up the coursework.

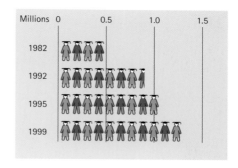

▲ Growth in the number of university students.

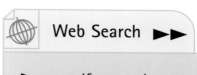

Web Search ▶▶

▶ www.dfee.gov.uk
Statistics and other information from Britain's Department for Education and Training.

Sports and Leisure

Many of the world's most famous sports began in Britain, including cricket, golf, soccer, and rugby. Horse-racing is another important spectator sport. In their leisure time, the British enjoy a range of pastimes, including hiking, cycling, golf, and bowls.

To many, soccer is Britain's national sport, and some of its teams are world famous, including Manchester United, Arsenal, and Liverpool. The domestic season runs from August to May. Regular fans attend matches at stadiums around the country, while international games attract huge TV audiences. In 2000, nearly half of Britain's population tuned in to watch England play Germany at Wembley Stadium in London.

Rugby originated at Rugby School in Warwickshire. Today, there are two versions of the game: rugby league has 13 players on each team, and rugby union has 15. The Welsh, in particular, are keen rugby union players, and key clubs include Cardiff, Swansea, and Neath.

Golf, horse-racing, and tennis

Scotland is traditionally regarded as the home of golf and England as the home of tennis. The most important golf club in Scotland, at the seaside town of St Andrew's near Dundee, has regularly hosted the British Open Championship since 1873. The world's most famous tennis club, at Wimbledon in London, hosts a major international tennis tournament each summer.

The key horse-racing events are the Derby, held at Epsom in Surrey, and the Grand National steeplechase held at Aintree, just outside Liverpool. Another equestrian sport is polo, brought to Britain from India in the 19th century by army officers. One of the most famous polo players is Prince Charles, the heir to the throne of Great Britain.

▲ Bowls is a traditional British sport. It is played both indoors and outdoors.

▲ International soccer is played at large stadiums across the country, including the Millenium Stadium in Cardiff. National competitions include English, Scottish, and Welsh leagues and championships.

Thousand Members

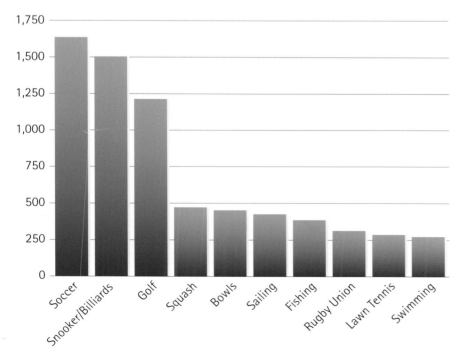

◄◄ Number of people belonging to sports clubs.

Web Search ►►

► www.culture.gov.uk
Government department for Culture, Media, and Sport.

► www.sportengland/org
www.ssc.org.uk
www.sports-council-wales.co.uk
Sports bodies of England, Scotland, Northern Ireland, and Wales.

Daily Life and Religion

I n Britain, the usual working and school weeks run from Monday to Friday, with the weekend free for leisure. The working day usually runs from 9:30 a.m. to 5:30 p.m., but many people work flexible hours, night shifts, and weekends.

Television is the main form of relaxation. Adults spend an average of nearly 2.5 hours a day watching TV or listening to the radio. Shopping is a popular weekend pastime. People shop at local markets, large downtown shopping malls, or out-of-town superstores.

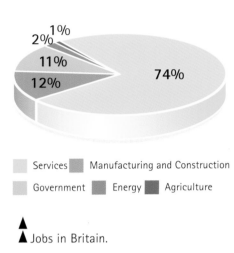

Services ■ Manufacturing and Construction
Government ■ Energy ■ Agriculture

▲ Jobs in Britain.

People shop at Petticoat Lane street market in London. ▼

Religion

The official religion of Great Britain is the Anglican Church, or Church of England. Almost 68 percent of the population are registered as Anglicans, and 22.5 percent as Roman Catholics. Other Christian groups include Presbyterians (particularly in Scotland), Methodists (particularly in Wales), and Baptists. Britain has the second-largest Jewish community in Europe. There are growing communities of Muslims, Hindus, and Sikhs.

Health care

Public health care is provided by the National Health Service (NHS), set up by the government in 1948. People can visit their family doctors and also receive free hospital treatment. Dentists and opticians provide free care only for people on low incomes, for children, and for senior citizens. There are also private hospitals and doctors. These are paid for mostly by medical insurance, which some companies provide for the benefit of their employees.

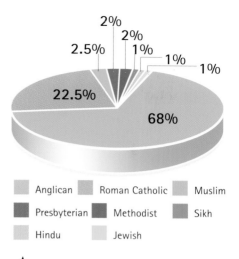

2%
2%
2.5%
1%
1%
1%
22.5%
68%

Anglican   Roman Catholic   Muslim
Presbyterian   Methodist   Sikh
Hindu   Jewish

▲ Number of people registered for different religions. Many of them do not practice their religion.

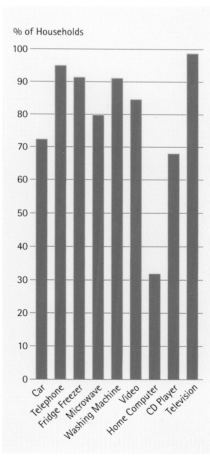

% of Households

▲ Ownership of appliances in Britain.

▲ Towns such as Winchester in England are built around an historic cathedral.

Arts and Media

Britain produces world-class newspapers, books, and television programs. Its musicians play on one in five of all recordings made worldwide, and theaters are flourishing. As well as world-famous galleries and museums, Britain has many small art collections.

Millions of people travel to Britain each year, visiting art galleries and theaters. *The Mousetrap*, a play based on an Agatha Christie novel, has been staged for over 40 years. It is the world's longest-running theater production. The Cardiff and Edinburgh International Festivals, spectacular celebrations of dance, music, and literature, are just two of many culture events that take place all over the country.

A crowd of tourists and local people watch a street performer at the Edinburgh Festival. ▼

 Web Search ►►

► **www.britishtourist authority.org**
Includes direct links to all Britain's tourist attractions.

► **www.scotlandonline. com/entertainment**
Features the latest exhibitions, concerts, and movie reviews for Scotland.

► **www.resource.gov.uk**
Britain's museum website.

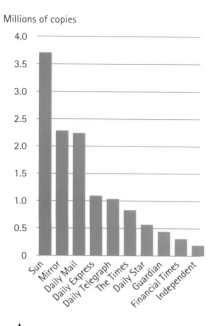

Millions of copies

A higher proportion of British people read newpapers than any other nation in the world.

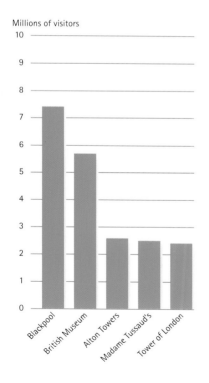

Millions of visitors

Movies and literature

The movie industry in Great Britain is thriving once again. It was world-famous in the 1930s and 1940s. Alfred Hitchcock, one of the greatest film directors of all time, was born in London. Many movies have been based on the works of the British writers William Shakespeare and Charles Dickens. Famous British poets include Dylan Thomas, William Wordsworth, and Robert Burns.

Television and newspapers

The publicly funded British Broadcasting Corporation (BBC) broadcasts two television channels, and its many radio stations include five national stations and the World Service. ITV, Channel 4, and Channel 5 are independent TV channels. There are many commercial radio stations. British viewers can also receive satellite and cable TV programs from all over the world.

Britain has more than 100 daily newspapers. The most famous are The Times, the Mirror, the Sun, and the Guardian. The biggest-selling regional paper is the Scottish Glasgow Daily Record (circulation 714,636). There are hundreds of magazines for both adults and children.

◄◄ Millions of people visit Britain's museums, castles, theme parks, and estates. Most foreign tourists come from the USA, Europe, and Japan.

DATABASE

World–Famous Performing Arts Institutions
- Birmingham Philharmonic Orchestra
- English National Opera
- Royal Ballet Company
- Royal Shakespeare Company
- Scottish Opera
- National Eisteddfod Society

Museums and Galleries
- Ashmolean Museum, Oxford
- British Museum, London
- Hayward Gallery, London
- Museum of Scotland, Edinburgh
- National Museum of Wales, Cardiff
- Scottish National Gallery of Modern Art, Edinburgh
- Tate Modern, London
- Tate, Liverpool
- Victoria and Albert Museum, London

Chronology of Historical Events

A.D. 43
The Romans invade Britain

500s
Angles, Saxons, and Jutes settle

600s
Viking raids

1066
Norman Conquest

1215
Magna Carta is signed

1536
England and Wales formally united

1601
James VI of Scotland inherits English throne from Elizabeth I and becomes King James I

1640s
English Civil War

1707
Act of Union between Scotland and England

1776
United States gains independence from Britain

1780s–1800s
Industrial Revolution

1800s
The British Empire expands

1801
Ireland is made a part of the United Kingdom

1922
Republic of Ireland gains independence

1999
Welsh national assembly and Scottish parliament are formed

Place in the World

In 1900, Great Britain was the center of the British Empire, a group of colonies all over the world. By 1970, Britain had lost almost all of its territories abroad, and its influence weakened. Despite this, Great Britain retains a role in world politics.

Britain's empire did not simply disappear. In 1931, it became the Commonwealth, an association of countries around the world formerly ruled by Britain, including Australia, India, Canada, Nigeria, and Jamaica.

Britain has a permanent seat on the Security Council of the United Nations (UN). Along with the United States and the Soviet Union, Britain led the way in founding this organization at the end of World War II. The UN's purpose is to maintain world security, and it has peace-keeping forces in many troubled parts of the world.

Members of the British royal family in 2000, including Queen Elizabeth II and the Queen Mother (center) and Prince Charles (second from right). All members of the royal family act as ambassadors for Britain overseas. ▼

▲ Oxfam, a British relief aid organization, works with NATO forces in Kosovo.

NATO and the EU

Britain was also a founding member of the North Atlantic Treaty Organization (NATO), a military alliance between the United States and several European countries that has existed since 1949.

Britain joined the European Economic Community (later renamed the European Community) in 1973. Today, an overall community of western European nations known as the European Union (EU) works towards greater cooperation between all the member countries. It allows free movement of tourists, exchange of students and workers, and encourages trade between members.

Although half of Britain's trade is with other EU countries, the United States remains Britain's single biggest trading partner. Many British people think of themselves as separate and different from continental Europeans.

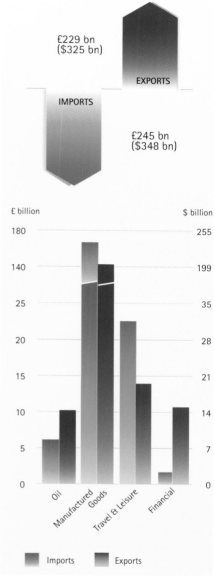

▲ Imports and exports—selected major categories.

Web Search ▶▶

▶ **www.open.gov.uk/pro/ prohome.htm**

Website of the Public Record Office, which holds government documents from A.D. 1066 to the present day.

Area:
88,800 sq mi (229,991 sq km)

Population size:
57,133,900

Capital city:
London (population 7,074,300)

Longest river:
Severn (220 miles (354 km))

Highest mountain:
Ben Nevis (4,406 feet (1,343 m))

Largest lake:
Loch Lomond (27 sq mi (71 sq km))

Flag:
The countries that make up Britain each have their own flag. England's is a red cross on a white background, and Scotland's, a diagonal white cross on a blue background. The Welsh flag features a red dragon on a green and white background. The UK's national flag is the Union Jack, which combines the crosses of St. George of England (red on white), St. Andrew of Scotland (diagonal white on blue), and St. Patrick of Ireland (diagonal red on white).

▲ Stonehenge, a prehistoric circle of stones on Salisbury Plain, southern England.

Official language:
English

Currency:
Pound sterling (£)

Major resources:
Oil, gas, coal, tin, limestone, iron ore, salt, clay, chalk, gypsum, lead, and silica

Major exports:
Manufactured goods, machinery, fuels, chemicals, transportation equipment, and financial services

National holidays and major events:
New Year's Day (January 1),
Holocaust Day (January 27),
St. David's Day (March 1),
Oxford v. Cambridge University
   Boat Race (last week in March),
Good Friday, Easter Sunday, and
   Easter Monday (March or April),
Grand National horse-race (first
   Saturday in April),

St. George's Day (April 23),
Early May Bank Holiday
   (first Monday in May),
Spring Bank Holiday
   (last Monday in May),
Queen's official birthday (June),
Royal Ascot (mid-June),
Royal National Eisteddford of
   Wales (early August),
Edinburgh Festival (August),
Summer Bank Holiday (August),
Notting Hill Carnival
   (last weekend in August),
Highland Games (early September),
Guy Fawkes' Day (November 5),
Remembrance Day (Sunday nearest
   November 11),
St. Andrew's Day (November 30),
Christmas Day (December 25),
Boxing Day (December 26),
New Year's Eve/Hogmanay
   (December 31)

Religions:
Anglican, Roman Catholic, Muslim, Presbyterian, Methodist, Sikh, Hindu, and Jewish

Glossary

AGRICULTURE
Farming.

ARABLE
Used for growing crops rather than raising livestock.

BIRTH RATE
The number of live births in one year per 1,000 women of childbearing age.

CLIMATE
The range of weather in a region over time.

COMMUTE
To repeatedly make the same journey from one particular place to another.

CURRICULUM
A program of study.

DEATH RATE
The number of deaths in a year per 1,000 of the population.

ECONOMY
The organization of a country's money and resources.

EMPIRE
A group of colonies ruled by a single country.

ETHNIC
Belonging to a particular race or culture.

EXPORTS
Goods sold to a foreign country.

FERTILE
Suitable for growing crops.

GOVERNMENT
The organization that sets and enforces laws for one nation.

GROSS DOMESTIC PRODUCT (GDP)
The total value of all the goods and services produced by a country in a year.

IMPORTS
Goods bought from a foreign country.

MANUFACTURING
Using machinery to make products from raw materials.

MONARCH
A hereditary head of state.

NATIONAL ASSEMBLY
An assembly of elected representatives that governs a country.

NATIVE
Belonging naturally to a place.

PARLIAMENT
A seat of government. The UK parliament is divided into the House of Commons and the House of Lords.

POLLUTION
Damage to the environment.

POPULATION DENSITY
The average number of people living on a particular area of land.

PRINCIPALITY
A territory controlled by a prince, in the same way that a kingdom is controlled by a king or queen.

PROVINCE
A part of a country or state that has a particular identity.

QUARRY
A site where rock is dug or blown out of the ground.

RESOURCES
A country's supplies of energy, natural materials, and minerals.

RURAL
Relating to the countryside.

SUBJECT
(1) An area of study, for example at school; (2) a person ruled over by a monarch.

URBAN
Relating to towns and cities.

Index